Ghost Policy

By LB Sedlacek

Acknowledgments

"Footle" was originally published in *Online Open Mic – Ponder Savant, March 2021*

"Frigid Water" was originally published in *Online Open Mic – Ponder Savant, March 2021*

"Gastrine Mill" was originally published in *Online Open Mic – Ponder Savant, March 2021*

"Graffiti Trail" was originally published in *Al-Khemia Poetica, March 2021*

"Hotel Sewing Kits" was originally published in *Alien Buddha Zine, 2021*

"No Cash Calls" was originally published in *Lone Stars Magazine #96, June 2021*

"Personal Movement" was originally published in *Clare, Spring 2015*

"Small Town Heroes" was originally published in *Lone Stars Magazine, March 2021*

"Unused Headshots" was originally published in *Al-Khemia Poetica, March 2021*

"Voice Lesson" was originally published in *Alien Buddha Zine, 2021*

Contents

A Ghost Afraid of Aging 7

Chalk Experience 9

Times Zero 10

Animal Soup 11

Immaculate Flavors 13

The Chin Up Position 14

Crunching Order 15

Ghost Policy 16

How to Rebuild a Human 17

Sampling Lipsticks 20

Counter…measured 21

Jumping From a Moving Train 22

Swift 23

Car Logic 24

Time Mural 25

Geographical Facts 26

Boundaries 27

The Hallway 28

A Sort of Cartography For Fools 29

Protected Left Turns 31

Heat Source 32

Super Seagrass 33

Tock 34

Graffiti 36

A Fish Tale 37

Rewind at the Carwash 38

Exchanging Umbrellas 39

One Way Symphony 40

The Reorganization of a Hum 41

Seeing is Believing 42

The Instructions For Showers 43

Farewell Mission 44

Patriotic Characteristics 45

The Attributes of Paper Clips 47

Most Unwanted Man 48

Hotel Sewing Kits 49

Voice Lesson 50

Frigid Water 51

Footle 53

Gastrine Mill 54

Graffiti Trail 55

Unused Headshots 56

Small Town Heroes 57

Chokeberry 58

Huckleberry Finn 60

Lunch Specials at the Bakery 62

Saint's Inheritance 63

Technical Reproduction 64

Day Vision 65

Crystal Ark 66

Way, Side, In 67

Bone Collection 68

Powder and Aftershave 69

The Synthespian Blues 70

Wardriving 71

LZW Algorithm 72

The Ghost of the Sun 73

Rust 74

The Lawnmower Symphony 75

Mermaid's Tears 76

Somebody's Mirror 77

Montana Mustangs 78

Neighborhood Watch 79
No Cash Calls 80
Notes on Postcards 81
A One Degree Change in Temperature 83
Personal Movement 85
Reinventing The Piano 86
Picnic Game 87
A Pillow and a Sunbeam 88
Rapid Cooling 89
Red Bows Saluting at Sixteen Feet 91
Refused 92
Rock Work 93
Roof Cement 95
Sawdust Origins 96
Invisibility School 97
About the Author L.B. Sedlacek 98
ALSO BY LB SEDLACEK 99

A Ghost Afraid of Aging

I. Brain Cocktail

I cannot pluck the stars from
the sky; or anywhere not even
off a dead pine tree
or scraped with a fingernail
off a notebook full of
science notes, historical
facts, algebra – it really isn't
good for anything, is it? —,
phone numbers, stock margins.
My head aches from the back where
I nicked the wall — an
accident, one of many; even
greasing the joints with vodka,
red wine loosens nothing but
flesh, and stars I did not see.
I close my eyes. This is not my home.

II. Cigarette Halo

A sprinkle of ash
along the ground
violent crumbs
of indigestion
or belches of
confession repressed
hallucinations

of lime green walls
TV's on stilts
polka dot paradise
replaced with
lost names
on crinkled
yellow paper
stuffed in shoe boxes
under the bed.

Chalk Experience

A child, maybe seven years old,
drawing
pictures, words, any old thing. It was
green — that I remember, and the chalk
was white. There's a rainbow of color
available, but the surface remains black
or green. Numbers were invincible. But
then they took it away, my little green
chalkboard, and my mother told me it was
by accident. I never had another
one after that.

Times Zero

I don't want to have to learn how to give anyone insulin
not even myself cause I'm afraid of needles even
the smallest ones and I get faint at the sight of
blood. How will I ever learn to do it? To prick
the skin, monitor the dosage, administer at
the right time of day every day? To leap
forward it will become a familiar
habit joining my toothbrush, my hairbrush,
my washcloth like they're all old friends
like they're all standing between existence
and any part of what used to be familiar.

Animal Soup

The rope wound in a coil,
hangs on the wall.
A thin nail extends its hand
its skin rough with rain.

It seems to say, "Believe in my strength,
believe in my direction."

He sits on a bale of hay
eating a sandwich. Hair
wild with wind and the
scent of insubordination.

His boots are clean,
his hands free of calluses,
his cowboy hat brand new.

The rope sprung from prison
whips in the air.
A thin neck takes its burden
its bones brittle with youth.
It cries in neighs and whinnies
"I will not stick around,
I'll leave footprints behind."

He stands whistling in the
corner. Hands and feet on
the corral. He takes a knife
and slices the rope into –

his hat drops to
the ground and rolls
and rolls some more then
around for a while.

Immaculate Flavors

A handprint in dust
is like that first kiss
in a bathroom closet
during a game of "Truth
or Dare" or maybe "Spin
the Bottle." Slurs and slangs
are thrown about in the
cafeteria halls so the geeks
stay separated from the cool
kids. An unwanted hand placed
between childish games splits
us all into pairs of
condiments, spices, sauces
and dressings – each one with
different tastes, different
expiration dates.

The Chin Up Position

Your body in an L shape
with
your back

against the wall
with
your feet

against the other wall
push
up with your hands

with your foot on the
opposite
wall. Rest. Repeat.

Alternate feet. When you
reach
the top, roll your weight

onto your forearms. Shift your
weight
to your hands.

Press up. Rest.
Repeat.
Alternate feet.

Crunching Order

The train whistle
belts
a hollow tune

from the mouth
behind
the

wooden whistle
heard at
the right

distance or
the perfect
moment

able to fool
everyone
or just

someone
into stopping
and looking

both ways.

Ghost Policy

sit on down
across the desk
dressed in your
best
and let's discuss
your
options:
invisibility
flying
helpful, happy, horror
classical howls and moans
or
giggles, chuckles
chains
not
included
optional decision –
how you want to die
note to client:
the messier,
the scarier

How to Rebuild a Human

Make sure there are
no visible wounds
check diet
check pulse
check liquid intake
feed at regular
intervals
next pop in
needles
to check fluids
and then record
everything
keep a chart
of
everything
maintain weight
maintain movement
maintain muscle mass
have fun
activities
planned throughout
the day
bird watching
dog watching
cat watching
reading
writing
sleeping
talking on the phone

make sure
there are 2 snacks
a day
rebuild wardrobe
rebuild toys
rebuild skin
rebuild hair
rebuild legs
rebuild arms
rebuild face
rebuild cosmetics
pants, shirts, socks
coats, shoes
bandit machines
stress poppers
brush, comb, mouthwash
toothpaste, toothbrush
and oh yes
learn to walk
learn to eat
learn to speak
again
be sure to place
enemy robots
on the other side
of the wall
behind cameras
and beware
of trusted friends
who become
your foes
because they have

slipped to the
wrong side
(promises, promises)
all of this is
in your manual
you never got
you can always
contact anyone
in the Directory
for help
(the Directory that
doesn't exist)
you will be tired
but you should be
proud –
you put a
human
back together

again.

Sampling Lipsticks

The cases are round and black
with plastic doorbells and haunting
shadows made of soap and sweat.

With hands sheathed in
crisp leather sheets, thick
dumpsters housing swimming pools.

Murky water seeps through the
cracks. My toes are damp.
The plastic chairs drip with water.

The sun comes out and
glints on the mirror situated
just behind me, a bit to the left.

Counter...measured

Counter espionage a little unusual
from behind the dings of a cash
register, the strain of varicose veins,
the stretch from the back, wrist
braces a web-filled armor for stocking
shelves, the items upon them neatly
harmless until mixed at a spy's
dance, a little cha cha spin leap
dip imaginative enthusiastic
technique and steps turning cold medicine
lethal information valuable as simple
as phone numbers for sale that can be
discovered in any phone books
the facts observed by simply
driving by someone anyone's
own front yard.

Jumping From a Moving Train

Jump from the last car.

Wait
for the
train

to slow
if you have time.

Pick a landing spot.
(Final decision?)
Soft.
No
obstructions.
(Your choice.)

Bend your knees and get low.
(Whatever it takes.)

Get perpendicular and leap as far
as possible.
(Gotta start somewhere.)

Roll.
Cover your
head
with your
arms

and pray.

Swift

A pencil gone awry, or the Mississippi's curves
squiqqled lines like oozing felt ink
bleeding through paper. The bullet
shaking, it lands in the mud. Chopin belts
out Muzak. Children giggle and cover their
ears. The hand bell slips from his fingers
punching him in the nose. A slight
mist
roars along the riverbanks. The
children
clap their hands, throwing pebbles into
the stream. Chopin's notebook floats
to the top, the words evaporated
along
with the children's voices that no
longer carry on the water's back.

Car Logic

Kings, kingdom
play, phylum
chess, class
on, order
funny, family
green, genes
squares, species
reminds me of
batteries, belts
charge, carburetor
engines, exhaust
vom, volt-ohmmeter.

Time Mural

A clock that won't skip
a single second in a
billion years, a brilliant
most accurate timepiece
using atoms' vibrations
producing a time standard.

To be more accurate
the atoms have to be
slowed down and counted.

No winding, no watch
band, no batteries.

A stable clock.

Geographical Facts

A secret history of Canada
invented by Thompson
and Small, the largest
pre-Confederation fur trade
marriage known – 58 years
of crossing the Rockies.

This accomplished map
maker (Thompson), this Cree
daughter of a fur trader (Small) —
they traveled farther than
Lewis & Clark in search of
passage to the Pacific.

The great map complete.

Boundaries

The pink tape
flaps
in the wind

so sure of
itself
and the boundaries

it marks. The
blue
tape is strewn

in the trees
almost
confetti, silly string

spewed along trip
wires
or lasers so

the feet can
be
put in the

right place never
stepping
over any lines.

The Hallway

In the lull after the sermon
the burgundy floor comes alive
a little girl gets a cup of ice
an old woman goes to the bathroom
an old man gets off the elevator
shuffling across the room with a cane.

It is the same ritual I see
on Sundays.

I sit in the back away
from it all, silently uninvolved.

A Sort of Cartography For Fools

When I was little my Dad used to
take me
grocery shopping in the brand new store
just built off the highway, and inside the
fruits and vegetables and breads all tucked
away in a section that looked like a house
with windows and a shingled roof decorated
for the holidays, the seasons.

The store still stands, the house section
removed, the lights not so bright, the
groceries downgraded to cheaper items,
store brands, maybe imports and
crowded which it never was when I first
started going, when the store had a different
name. We used to grind our own coffee.
I liked that the best.

Our neighbor never shopped at the old
grocery store and now he doesn't know
how. He can't drive, not because he
doesn't know how, but because he
can't remember. Spots of his old self
shine through, he knows but he doesn't know.
Where did his mind go wrong?
And it happened just exactly like it says
in article descriptions right down
to the mental fog making me wish
this was only thrust upon liars. They

deserve to have their mental state wiped
clean, the words torn from their mouths
so the rest of us aren't left holding a
flashlight searching for the human
beings we used to know.

Protected Left Turns

Two rows of trailers stacked like a
movie set
with spotlights in the dark but there's nothing
entertaining about it or the flow of traffic
creeping behind a refinery plant stuck in the
middle of the city bleeding fumes along with
the traffic backed up from here to there making
me wonder back to my grandparents and
their farm and wonder what they would think
— if they could see it now – of all this progress.

Heat Source

Undyed
untaxed
Kerosene.

Nontaxable
use
only.

Almost
as bad
as a
bee sting.

You
shouldn't
use Kerosene
for that.

Super Seagrass

Submerged meadows
in serious decline
around the world
close allies
with water fowl
depending on it for food.
Grass beds generating oxygen.
Sometimes they fizz
with bubbles. They offer
shelter from predators, thick
enough to protect from a
fishing net. Absorbs
pollution. Fights crime.
Leaps small buildings in
a single bound. Holds
open the door for strangers.
5 acres of it
can sequester the carbon
dioxide from an
automobile.

Tock

Traffic stopped (and maybe time too)
on the highway just below
the Blue Ridge Mountains.

The day glorious, weather
perfect (slight hint of sun and clouds,
sky, no rain) except for being
stopped. We climbed out of our
cars trying to figure out what
was going on (slight hint of that
from the fire truck, the ambulance,
the emergency rescue vehicle),
talked to our neighbor drivers
on their way home like us
with our destination only 200
feet away and in sight.

We exchanged information, name dropped,
shared opinions on why no lines of traffic
were moving, watched a guy hike
up the road to use the Porta-John
parked on the side due to the
construction going on to make the 2
lane a 4 lane. The woman in
front of us took off her shoes, opened
her trunk, shifted stuff around. A
guy came up to us sharing a slight
hint of what had happened. A woman on
a motorcycle struck straight on

by a white van. She was pinned
underneath. The plan to Medivac
her out, but the helicopter never came.

The fire truck, ambulance,
emergency rescue vehicle drove
past us one by one, and we could
see traffic start to move.

I looked out at the mountains,
the hills, the sky, the blue
thinking at least she went out
with a view.

Graffiti

The library book encased in plastic
laminated
from smudgy hands
wears and tears
inside a label
attached
warning that it's a
crime to mar
the inside, a piece of
paper glued
there with lines
for initials or names
or doodles.

I've checked out books
before with words, sentences
underlined in
pen and pencil
corners earmarked as
if to say someone was here.

Yeah, someone was here.

A Fish Tale

Fishing nets dipped in lakes
or a wet towel drying
in the sun can cool
down bottles of wine when
there's no ice, no freezer,
no refrigerator, nothing
but a man-made lake
and a house built to look
200 years old for feet to
perch up on the porch
railings, hair blowing
in the wind with a fishing
pole dangling in the water
to catch fish and then release
prompting one to consider
if fish could think wonder
what they'd think of us?

Rewind at the Carwash

There's nothing like that first car,
I'd rather forget what I had,
some off the wall brand, a stick shift,
not as nice as the red truck the
boy with the black hair is driving.
He sits in front of me at the car
wash. Jumps out of the car removing
things from the back, taking off the
antennae. He's in and out of the
car 4 or 6 times. It must be his
first time, I think. I giggle.

I laugh again. The red truck
goes forward, stops, forward again.
Stops at the red light, the washing
begins.

My turn now. The truck hasn't left the
parking lot. The boy – teenager all of
16? – steps out, walks around
examines the wash, his ride. I remember
it is Saturday night. If I was
younger,
single, no family, I might've been
out
washing my car for date night … too.

Exchanging Umbrellas

1)

A building and a room
and a broken umbrella
the handle falling off
the top caving in
rain drops pouring down the
forehead that doesn't blend
like black into the carpet
into the dark green walls
becoming a backdrop for
a floral forest.

2)

A building and a room
with a crowd so large

it's standing room only
human beings thread through
needles, human beings
thread through handshakes
grim faces or cool grins
participating in the ritual
so well-known to all
this treeless forest.

One Way Symphony

The leaves play a symphony as I look at
them from the front porch wondering as
many have before how they can be so
beautiful as they are dying
this perfect collage of
gold, yellow, red, pink, orange and
even green making music in the wind
unconcerned with the mist, haze and
dark clouds rolling in
unconcerned with how much
longer they might have to
sing a solo
unconcerned
unlike me
concerned with
everything so rushed I
hadn't noticed until now
this perfect collage of leaves
this perfect symphony of color
I hadn't noticed until now
when I decided to stop
pull out my earplugs
turn off my leaf blower and
listen for a few minutes
unconcerned
until I become concerned
again.

The Reorganization of a Hum

The hum is silent now.

It was soft like white
noise a subtle roar to
the ears so they would
know the factories were humming
along spitting out table tops,
desks, couches and chairs and
anything to fill a room
where a sometimes hum
might clear it.

For Sale signs large, white with red
letters screaming for help, but
no one's listening.

They don't hum overseas.

The factories churn out
anything to fill a room
but no one's buying it.

Seeing is Believing

A man who could be Santa Claus
drives a Ford SUV, green and brown,
and has an RV. He has reddish
skin, white hair and a beard, white too.
He parks the RV sometimes in
the church parking lot across the
street from his house. He banks at
the Bank of America and has an
old bumper sticker on the back of
his SUV for former Presidential
candidate Kerry.

I see him every day when I drive by
his house on the corner.

I know he never sees me.

The Instructions For Showers

Each one — different
Like all the ways to cook eggs:
Runny, Fried, Scrambled
Signals from radios, CB's
Seeking asylum from boredom
Or, desert droughts cured by
gallons
Of water or six-packs of beer
Swilled on Labor Day at Lake Havasu
With body bags more plentiful than
boats
Drifting from motel to motel
Scanning through each room manual
Only learning enough to use the shower.

Farewell Mission

Pantyhose, batteries and toothpaste.
The best sellers on holidays at
convenience stores. The stores, once
hopping, the shelves bare, the stock low,
the parking lot empty. The pallets are
empty too everything coming by boat,
made overseas, piled in containers so
full the wares sit in warehouses collecting
dust, cause it's cheaper to store than to
manufacture locally. The assembly lines
stand alone, jilted, silent. The sun –
homeless now — creeps in through the
painted windows (painted to keep eyes
from wandering) looking for another home.

Patriotic Characteristics

Curved ears set them apart.
The Marwari – mar-wah-ree.
Watchfulness, horse intelligence, in
every color except chestnut:
if a Marwari foal is barn
with a chestnut color it's a
mark that it has mixed
blood or Thoroughbred ancestry.
Popular but rare is the color
cremela (nukra), a cream
horse with blue eyes like
farmer's daughters with blonde
hair and flowing locks.

They mix with the crowd
of overalls or sombreros
or Polo shirts, eyes lifted
to the sky on the Fourth of
July fireworks reigning
over the bridge, the dry
riverbed (arroyo) in Dodge City,
Kansas, and elsewhere.

Gray Marwari are in the
greatest demand, their
ears curve so tightly they
cross in the middle.

They are fine-skinned, sure-
footed and devoted. There
are six thousand in India, ten in the
United States. They are
hot-tempered, never irrational.

The fireworks pop, their
sound sharply defined.

The Attributes of Paper Clips

Paper cups and magazines
strewn about
as calling cards on silver platters
introducing salt and water
to unsuspecting
bubble gum chewers
or bearded men
using fingers for words
the only consistent thing
is the box's ever-changing glare,
and the inexplicable reason
for a paperclip's invitation
to this dance of chest thumps
and eyelids sending Morse code
trying to send a signal
to
all the scattered puzzle pieces
so they can find their way
home again.

Most Unwanted Man

He doesn't swing from a vine.
His hands aren't swollen with
calluses. His hair is short
and crew cut and gray. He
squints when he looks
far away. Buxom women
with swizzle stick figures
don't swoon at his feet, or
when he takes his shirt off.
Predators don't run in fear.
He passes through any crowd
without a head turn or a
passing glance. His suit
is two sizes too big. His
shoes are scuffed at the toes.
He wears the same watch he's
worn for years. He parks his
car in the same spot in the
driveway: to the right,
underneath the sycamore
tree. He laughs at jokes that
aren't funny. His pockets are
full of phone numbers handed
to him by people who don't
know his name.

Hotel Sewing Kits

A flick of the wrist
a pinch of the fingers
weaving the thread thin long
into a button a tear
to fill a yearning gap
primary colors are one choice
sometimes there are other choices
how to decide to chose
the thread needs to last
the thread needs to hold
and it should be inconspicuous
a grab at the shoulders
a squeeze around the waist
too subtle might be unnoticed
and then there's the excitement
of the repair an apprentice
finally working on their own
a mentor who has succeeded
the thread, though, is binding
anyone ensnared can never leave
not that they want to.

Voice Lesson

I took voice lessons
sang in the choir
got a music scholarship
to college
never graduated
in music
did something else
more practical
a business degree
and I
wrote lyrics
hauling thick black
notebooks full
of songs
on notebook paper
and I
tried recording
tried forgetting
but later
in a job
helping kids
they let me
play the drum
and I
was in their band
and I
got to sing some backup
it was the closest
I ever got
to being a singer.

Frigid Water

(1) Don't attempt to swim.

Holed up in a basement with physics
students transmitting data using
a telegraph's electronic circuits.

(2) If you have a life vest, put it on.

December 15, 1955 - some say it
was the first time a computer
remotely transmitted data.

(3) Pull yourself tight into a ball to
retain body heat.

A 33 year old telegrapher for the
Canadian National Railway took a leap
into modern day computer networking.

(4) If you don't have a life vest, grab
anything that floats.

This data exchange saved months
of calculations all with the push of
a button.

(5) If someone else is with you,
huddle together for warmth.

A small first step to get computers
to operate together.

(6)If you don't have a floatation device,
float on your back or tread water
very slowly.

With only a half megabyte of memory
it solved engineering problems.

(7)When rescued, check for signs of
hypothermia.

Natural computer calculations.

Signs of severe body heat loss are
slurred speech and no shivering.

Slowly re-warm your body.

Footle

We talk
act foolishly
as if
nothing's wrong
as if
wires, plugs
are normal
connected to
the body
to keep
it breathing
lissome, fair
even as
the organs
shut down.

Gastrine Mill

Lobsters have teeth in their stomachs
for chewing their food
(even at their last meal)
a fact about as strange
as coffee on ceiling tiles
or houses sitting on triangle lots
or detached mothers watching their
kids play at the park.

Imagine that lobster enjoying a
three course dinner
on the ocean floor
(or maybe a last meal)
swimming around in a giant fish tank
without a way to escape
a fact about as real
as the sandwich generation
a fatal diagnosis
a missing person found alive.

It's always better to chew food
thoroughly 'cause you don't know
when you will eat again,
(the last meal).

Graffiti Trail

Paint can caps
of neon
orange, blue
forgotten in the sand and a
pink jacket hanging
on a pole
forgotten
this road to the lighthouse
chained off
the abandoned lighthouse far out in
the sea inaccessible but you
can still see it from the
beach they must come at night to spray paint to
graffiti the
roadway, the parking lot with
so and so plus so and so
motivational messages
drawings
in orange, blue, pink, yellow
and red
the lighthouse, untouched, stands tall
and takes the sea in
a blend of grays
lacking in spray paint, no graffiti, no color.

Unused Headshots

The manila envelope could contain
anything: a passport, a wallet,
someone's keys, ad copy, a book,
an important memo, a secret recipe
this manila envelope contains
headshots taken 20 years ago
forgotten and closed up inside
a silent tomb of facial youth
this manila envelope contained
too much hair and bushy eyebrows
a mole or two, long since removed
lipstick that's no longer worn
this manila envelope contained
hairspray that's no longer used
a suit jacket with shoulder pads
heavy makeup so out of vogue
this manila envelope contained
dreams of acting, singing, modeling
a skinny body devoured by age
a three second chance at stardom
this manila envelope contains
an unsellable photograph
a face with no wrinkles
natural colored hair
the manila envelope could contain
something: hope, innocence, dreams,
imagination, desire, achievement,
success or a secret romance

but now this manila envelope contains
unused headshots worth nothing at all.

Small Town Heroes

Childhood friends keep popping up
in places
unexpected – the hospital, the library
the school carnival with their kids
and we were supposed to have
all grown up and moved away and
become successful. Instead; we are
here where we started. Some
never left. Some moved
away and came back.
Nothing as exciting as a trip to
the moon — a reentry to
earth a rare achievement. There's no
climbing of the social ladder, no
stunts to pull, no impressive stories
to tell. It's just the same as it was
with age. Some people like
waking up every day invisible.

Chokeberry

72 hours
3 days
isn't that long
but when
avoiding
something
anything
such as
napkins flapping
in the window
of a dark
restaurant

a ghost at tea
a gremlin doing shots
a gargoyle sipping a latte'

a plant at the zoo
a missing fishing lure
a singing cowboy

72 hours
3 days
not enough time
to think of
a proper excuse
to avoid a
class reunion
such as

hiking in Switzerland
hurling along the zipline
hanging 10 in the surf

who would
believe any of
it anyway?

Huckleberry Finn

He was what he was.
Free spirit.
Strong resistance.
Uncivilized.
Brought up without any rules.
A natural life:
brown maple,
brown mud Mississippi.
Wouldn't wear new clothes.
Wouldn't give up smoking.
Wouldn't learn the Bible.
Straw hat.
Straw scarecrows.
Overalls.
Bare feet.
Over all.
Freckled face.
Honorable thief.
Pirate. Buccaneer.
Freebooter phenomenon.
Hungry.
Superstitious.
Brought up on the land.
Sarcastic.
Scoffed at religion.
Tom Sawyer's pirate friend.
Uncorrupted. Uncomplicated.
Fabulously wealthy.
Frivolous fable.

Allegorical odds and ends.
Like a shipwrecked boat,
a graveyard apparition:
he did what he did.

Lunch Specials at the Bakery

The dance of split indecision
is a facial recognition
hair, body type, voice,
walk, dress, movements
and then instant decision
to speak a greeting
a hand wave
a nod or to look eyes
down at your meat loaf
your pimento cheese sandwich
to think instead upon
the baked goods locked
in the glass display
to make a choice
of a pastry, cookie or
slice of pie or cake
all the while trying to
stay connected to the
outside world everyone
else pretends to forget.

Saint's Inheritance

The approach should be
subtle at first as a lemon

bathing in water

skinny dipping with like
minded ice cubes swilling

back ten-gallon burnished

browns, glasses for the ladies,
bottles for the men who

sit back a tip-tapping toes

to their cardboard radios
playing tunes in their heads,

and the ladies whisper to the

lemons offering favors in
exchange for explanation

of block letters that spell out

"Food Stamps Accepted" in black
and red on a white plastic sign.

Technical Reproduction

It looks like a round white bullet
except it's high atop an SUV,
and more like a bazooka gun.

I imagine inside plans to
build a house, a business, a
structure so rare that the container
had to go on that roof
of that SUV, had to
be secured outside the car for easy
quick retrieval
almost protecting itself
from the troubles ahead: a deed
search, rights to sewer, power and
water, rights to a driveway that
connects to the main road.

All these rights seem so easy
in a canister on top of the roof
of an SUV unless there really

is a bazooka gun inside.

Day Vision

On a freeway in England
slightly south of London,
up on a hillside.
It had just stopped raining.
Your car was stopped under
the electric power lines.

You were standing with your
thumb out and didn't move
when I stopped my car behind yours.
Steam poured from the engine.
The air smelled of wet tires.

You held your finger to your
lips, and pointed to the sky.
"You affect the light by your
proximity." I stepped a
little closer and considered hugging you.

Later in the evening, the tow
truck came and we followed
in my sedan your head turned
back all the while as you
muttered "we are better
conductors than glass tubes."

Crystal Ark

Nunavik above Quebec
contains a crystal eye
a crater, pure water
no inlets, no outlets
one of North America's
deepest lakes
host to one of the most
unique biotic environs
on Earth
no hammocks
no dog walking paths
only uninterrupted sedimentation
zero food sources
an abundance of Arctic char
clear water
large and round
a drinking well for
a giant or something else
inhabiting surrounding tundra
or even a secret landing spot
for back end space exploration
gathering date on Earth
one of the most popular places
to buy cheap
chunks of paradise.

Way, Side, In

The past keeps crawling
back at me.

I claw it away
and it finds me
mail, email
making me remember
things I'd put in
built-in storage or
attic rooms
far away
from the moment.

I think of my response
to the past
the laughter
the hugs
any kisses?

I know more now.
I know repeating it
won't be the same,
a reunion not like
in my head.

I put the imagination
on autopilot forgetting
I was ever anywhere
before here.

Bone Collection

Bones mending
slotted together
steel metal hinges
circular slick
round
slotted together
fists up
like fingers
counting to ten
putting labels on straight
or slotted together
in hanging plastic bags
ready for pick up
ready to cure
knitting bones
mending bones
slotted together.

Powder and Aftershave

For history or finding roots
under rubble an odd little
twist, a surviving relic —
babies in the maternity lab
sleek and mirror bright
the whole story flushed by
scholars. An original state —
no genetic materials,
ancient images devoted
to people who live forever
as specimens preserved.
Break out the safari garments,
put away the space gear.
The headlines scream
we aren't interesting because
we're human, we're interesting
because we live. But still
we find ourselves alone, the pilot
seat empty.

The Synthespian Blues

3 months behind on child support and hours
down at the factory, my bank account closed cause of overdraft
fees
and all I have left is enough to fill
up with one tank of gas and buy some
groceries, I still have the power turned
on but I'm behind on that too, I sit in the dark and watch TV
and think how easy it would be to
have a digital face, words plugged
into my head, lips and arms and legs
plucked like puppet strings, and I
think of the court and my orders
and I think of how school was
supposed to teach me everything but
didn't and I think of the motorcycle
I had but sold so I could go to school,
so I could do all the things except
be there for my children when they need
me because I'm 3 months behind, I'm
short on hours at work, my bank
account's closed not that there's anything
to put in there anyhow anyway.

Wardriving

Armed with a laptop
(notebook) and GPS
cruising the cities in an
armored Chevrolet
(without an apple pie)
searching for those who
are unprotected, searching
for signals, searching for
connections available beyond
the walls. It's easy to be
anonymous in a Chevrolet
(without an apple pie) and
hook up (meet up, target)
an unsecured connection.
Access points. Signals.
Passwords. Encryption.
A little reminiscent of
war dialing — dialing
random numbers in search
of a modem. Encryption.
Passwords. Signals. Access.
Wireless. Hacker activity.
Security breaching. Insidious
tapping. Random break ins.
Mapping risk.

LZW Algorithm

French cuff shirts
and
hair down to there
tinted with gasoline
fire
to tinge hearts aflutter
and make chalk
an accessory
(isn't there some great play about chalk?)
to murder
but no crime
has been committed
(is it one to use a calculator?)
she said "yes"
while she was teaching
calculus
(I still haven't figured out what it's good for)
and threatening
to have us hanged
for
ending sentences with prepositions
and for
using our calculators
in the shadows
in our fantasies
trying
to inject our own histories
permanently.

The Ghost of the Sun

is simply the moon
loved by
typewriter
enthusiasts
causing pencils to be
sad
or kids to wonder
what one is even
if it has music
notation
the light, though, on
the
first floor green, white
a deep dark brown
either
sibling
the shadow of the sun
and yes now we
see
a
ghost

Rust

Rusty water tower
belonged to the factory
closed up
boarded up
used for a Haunted House
at Halloween
awaiting its repurpose
if it's too be

the railroad tracks run by
with ghost loads
what was made there
and who made it

surely the tower is empty
not filled with morsel drops
of rusty water
dripping down gray
metal sides
onto the tracks

the train roars by just now
as tree limbs hang on its doors
it will have to keep going
past the rusty water tower

it will have to keep going

The Lawnmower Symphony

The sound of the lawnmower is of
comfort to some, like the ding of the
microwave, the buzz of the alarm, the
din of the TV. All distractions taken
for granted unless time becomes finite
and saying goodbye the last choice left.

Mermaid's Tears

Polished shards of
faith, hope, charity
tossed about by
waves of
fortitude, justice
then thrown on
the beach by
prudence and
temperance.

You never know
what you will
find along the beach.

Somebody's Mirror

Discarded mirror in the trash
lambs jumping and playing
unexpected as dogs barking
behind fences one escaping
dashing down busy streets
stopping at yard's end
the day continues on
a flurry a whine
into the following day
that will too be
discarded as a mirror
was on a Tuesday.

Montana Mustangs

The mustangs are purple on a wall carpet
galloping along the hallway
nostrils flared and flowing purple manes
in fiber's attempt at reanimation.

Neighborhood Watch

Flowers wilted
in search of
rain

from dark clouds
rushing forward
to

the tune of
hammers, nails, bulldozers
all

the trappings of
a good neighborhood
that

makes no difference to
anyone except the
flowers.

No Cash Calls

A pay phone had this sign
No cash accepted for phone calls
Making me wonder how the bills
Would fit in the little coin slot.
North Pole Time Share

Predictions of Artic ice rebounding
the first time in 100,000 years
thin first ice covering the Artic Ocean
that didn't melt over summer but
instead grew larger than the same
time last year. With perfect
atmospheric storms melting ice
conditions approach rapid decline.
Artic Ocean ice-free summers.
Vacation brochures coming soon.

Notes on Postcards

Someone's trip to Europe is what a
postcard might say with an
obligatory "wish you were
here." No one writes
that anyway cause if they wished
it, there you'd be. It reminds me
of the downtown
department store. Seven stories
high. Endless rhythmic escalators
wide enough for one. We tapped our
feet watching pale yellow walls
transform into bedding, suits or
dresses. We tapped our fingers
waiting to land by the toys. On the
top floor, we ate hotdogs under
red and white umbrellas. On the
bottom floor, we ran in and out
of the revolving door
under watchful salesmen's glares.
When the luxury condos came,
we held our children's hands as the
walls were tossed into the street.
We ate hotdogs
from a street vendor just up the
corner away from the dust. The
mustard was bitter, the onions too sweet,
the chili burnt, the relish dried and tart.
We returned a lost dog to its home that
very same afternoon.

We didn't leave a note.
The owner
never
knew their pet was gone.

A One Degree Change in Temperature

Acquaintance keeps talking and
divulging her covert
operations. We are not
confidants or even associates.
She talks to me like we've
known each other for years.

The radio comes on and the
host, the DJ, whatever he is,
speaks of stalking a hot
celebrity. Maybe not
stalking, but spying from
his bathroom window, through
the trees. He says he can
hear her, voices carry.

Then the mail arrives
with its promises of
unseen footage, deleted
scenes, perfumes
and gardening tools.

There are books on outsmarting
squirrels, windmills to wipe
out moles, giant plastic hands
for scooping leaves, the
remedy for woebegone gardens.

Bambi & Company chew on
grass blades and weeds.
The doe inches towards my
tomato plants. When
she gets close enough, all
it takes is a drumming of
fingers on windows to send
her scurrying away.

Personal Movement

The factory turns out
black boxes
full of

thousands of pairs
of
shoes.

A few blocks away
someone goes
barefooted.

Reinventing The Piano

Two aspirin
And a Coke
Can't improve
The sound
Of ambidextrous hands
That get
Left mixed up
With right. Palm trees
In winter can't even
Shield
Cities from 6
Feet of snow. One
Candle is not enough
To light
A single room.
Yet, wax is strong enough
To hold it together –
Crayons, Chocolate, or
To polish cars
With large hands
For large SUV's.
When these two hands
Were smaller, they
Would've given anything
For that 64-pack
(88 keys) ecstasy
Wrapped up in colored
Paper: that
Bright
Orange box –
A coloring book's sonata.

Picnic Game

Cold fried homemade chicken
that's what I remember from
traveling and stopping at
rest stops, rest areas
and the cement picnic tables
set adrift amidst the
cars, cars with trailers and
trailer tractor parking lots
and sometimes they had a
shelter overhead. Our picnics
came out of a wooden basket
with paper plates, biscuits, cold
drinks. Back then, back 30 years
ago you couldn't find fast food
convenience store convenience.
It was easier to pack picnics.
It was cheaper to pack a picnic.
My sister hated the picnics
that's what I remember from
traveling and stopping at rest stops.
She was embarrassed we weren't
dining out (dining in) at any
restaurant. Me, I liked eating at
the picnic tables and the games of
tag or touch football after.
I liked eating cold fried chicken.
I liked stopping at rest areas.
I just liked being outdoors.

A Pillow and a Sunbeam

A little girl just three years old
shouldn't come between her Mom
and Dad but she did and she never
knew it, she simply wanted to follow
her Mommy crawling from the roaring
car revved into motion by tiny knees,
ankles, fists crawling out the open
door as unforgiving machinery
chewed up her parents splitting them
into, her Mother weeping in ankle deep
water, her Father locked away
a circus freak, and all it takes is
really the tiniest motion and its
effect on the tide, the ripple
that sends a leaf downstream, that
rips a road into with wild onions
stabbing at the cracks so thick
with blood, a perennial wasted
in green grass meadows under eternal
pear trees with a stone for a
pillow, a sunbeam for a blanket.

Rapid Cooling

They were like
dynamite
but

not delivered through
the
mail

fireworks that would
pop
in

the air (there's
some
law

against that now
in
this

state) and we
waited
for

them to arrive
like
snow

interrupting a school
day
or

the ice cream
truck
in

the summer. The
fireworks
made

now just aren't
the
same.

Red Bows Saluting at Sixteen Feet

Red bows hanging at 16 feet greet me at every bridge I pass
under
going 65, 70, or sometimes 55 mph in my borrowed SUV
with four brand new tires with thick wide tread
now giving me height above the asphalt – purpose behind the
wheel
that I never had in my car now sitting dormant under the shed
with a cracked window and a flat tire – still not beyond repair
all it needs is the right mechanic and a new tire … maybe two
except I've been through the yellow pages and
I can't find anyone who can fix it — not even temporarily
reducing me to borrowing vehicles with new tires and thick
treads
until I find a repairman who can cure my car for good.

Refused

Fourteen days was the wait
it was too long so short it
didn't happen, bodily harm
expiring without a single breath
and no dry eyes there to say
"hello" but there instead to
say "goodbye" unworried by
clerks shorting change
restaurants that won't take checks
used auto parts paid for as if they
were new. No parts to
be fixed, nothing to return,
nowhere to complain, a
life unspoiled, a life never lived.

Rock Work

I skipped a page
didn't want to leave it blank
so I went back
and began to fill it
while stopped in traffic
my legs aching all the while
it's not an injury
it's not arthritis
it's just aging
so I'm told
and I kept at the page
I couldn't leave it blank
I sat back
and tried to fill it
while stopped in traffic
behind a burgundy truck
with a horse trailer,
a yellow-orange service truck
with a burgundy ball cap
hanging on the back window,
and a burgundy Volvo
with a blue-yellow cross
Switzerland symbol
stuck on by the tag
and I almost finished the page
few spaces left to leave blank
I sat back and was glad I filled it.
I picked up the page
folded it into thirds

and zipped it up in my pocket
to unfold
to look at
to read
later.

Roof Cement

Pattern variation
as thick as
rain

slopping sidewalks
as thick as
caulk

oozing carefully
along the
seams.

Sawdust Origins

Sawdust piles floating at
feet scooped with old hands
new fingers a wonderful
sensation the tiny woodchips
float as confetti
confetti celebrates
the sawdust scatters
ashes tossed at sea
off mountain tops
left lingering in sealed metal
containers
confetti celebrates
the sawdust scatters
a tree's last breath
trimmed trunks to keep
the jolts flowing
confetti celebrates
the holly tree, a tiny limb
left in the sawdust piles
is all that remains
the sawdust scatters
across the empty lot
sun pouring on
trunks skimmed to the surface
exposed roots slowly dying
confetti celebrates
but the sawdust scatters
the trees we played beneath
are no more.

Invisibility School

The swing of the open sign —
the only clue
that someone, anyone,
is here at all,
this peg leg salad
of corn, peas, onions
and their lingering smell —
like unknown actors
performing a play
in front of empty seats.

About the Author L.B. Sedlacek

L.B. Sedlacek's poetry has appeared in publications such as "The Hill Rag," "Madness Muse Press," "Poesis," "Linerider Press," "As It Ought to Be," "Adelaide Literary Magazine," and others. Some of her latest poetry books are "I'm No Robot" (Cyberwit Press), "The Adventure of Stick People on Cars" (Alien Buddha Press), "Happy Little Clouds" (Guerilla Genesis Press), and "Words and Bones" (Finishing Line Press.) Her first short story collection, "Four Thieves of Vinegar & Other Short Stories" came out on Leap Day, 2020 from Alien Buddha Press. She teaches poetry at local schools, published the free resource for poets, "The Poetry Market Ezine," for 20 years and was a Poetry Editor for "ESC! Magazine." In her free time, LB enjoys swimming, reading, and playing the ukulele.

ALSO BY LB SEDLACEK

POETRY
Alexandra's Wreck - *Kitty Litter Press*
Happy Little Clouds – *Guerilla Genesis Press*
I'm No Robot - *Cyberwit*
Poetry in LA – *GoatsonMars Press*
Simultaneous Submissions - *Cyberwit*
The Architect of French Fries - *Presa Press*
The Blue Eyed Side - *Cyberwit*
The Poet Next Door - *Cyberwit*
Words and Bones - *Finishing Line Press*

FICTION
A Sunless Sea
Four Thieves of Vinegar & Other Short Stories - *Alien Buddha Press*
The Glass River
The Mailbox of the Kindred Spirit
Traveling with Fish

NON-FICTION
Bridge Ices Before Road
Electric Melt
The Catnip Gene
The Traveling Postcard